THEN & NOW

GREENSBORO

THEN & NOW

GREENSBORO

Lynn Salsi

For Burke Salsi Sr.

Copyright © 2007 by Lynn Salsi
ISBN 0-7385-4362-4

Library of Congress control number: 2006931405

Published by Arcadia Publishing
Charleston SC, Chicago IL, Portsmouth NH, San Francisco CA

Printed in the United States of America

For all general information contact Arcadia Publishing at:
Telephone 843-853-2070
Fax 843-853-0044
E-mail sales@arcadiapublishing.com
For customer service and orders:
Toll-Free 1-888-313-2665

Visit us on the Internet at www.arcadiapublishing.com

ON THE FRONT COVER: The images on the front cover show the dichotomy between preservation and growth—two things Greensboro leaders have balanced since 1900. This visual comparison of then and now only hints where Greensboro has been and where it will go. Organizations like Action Greensboro continue to be involved in revitalization along with preservation. Since 2000, downtown has undergone major improvements as old buildings are repurposed and public spaces beautified. (Photographs courtesy of the author.)

ON THE BACK COVER: In the past, Greensboro was a small town surrounded by vast farms of tobacco, cotton, and vegetables. Now there are no farms located near the city center. The few farms that are left are located within Guilford County rather than the city. However, Greensboro supports the small farmers with the operation of a farmer's market on Yanceyville Street and near the airport. (Historic photograph courtesy the Farrell Collection, North Carolina Office of Archives and History.)

CONTENTS

ACKNOWLEDGMENTS

Thanks goes to Burke Salsi for allowing his many outstanding "now" photographs to be used. Thanks to Les Seaver-Davis for sharing a portion of his archival photograph collection and to Jim Dollar for the use of his photographs.

I would also like to thank the following: Steve Massengill, archivist, historical consultant, and collector; Judy Morton, Action Greensboro; Kim Cumber, archivist, North Carolina Office of Archives and History; Stephen Catlett, archivist, Greensboro Historical Museum; Keith Longiotti, archivist, Wilson Library, University of North Carolina at Chapel Hill; Gwen Ericksen, Guilford College Library, the Quaker Collection; Cheryl Hemric, Guilford Technical Community College; April Hutchison, City of Greensboro; Jim Schlosser, *Greensboro New and Record* newspaper; Melody Watson, publicist; and Dianne and Julian McClamroch for family history.

I appreciate the help of the following friends and colleagues: Jan Hensley, Connie Mason, Barbara Springs, Glenn Bolick, Jim and Mary Young, Mary Kay Forbes, and Norma and Earl Thomas.

Thanks go to Maggie Bullwinkel of Arcadia Publishing.

David Weatherly and Roy Ackland of *Roy's Folks* at Fox 8 Television in High Point have provided encouragement for this project.

AUTHOR'S NOTE: The location of historical buildings was found in copies of city directories located in the Greensboro Public Library and with the help of Judy Morton, April Hutchison, and Jim Schlosser. Other verification was by micro fiche of archival newspapers in the library and from *Guilford North Carolina the County Seat of Guilford* by Ethel Stephens Arnett.

Unless otherwise noted, all photographs and illustrations are provided by the author from the Salsi family collection.

INTRODUCTION

Then & Now: Greensboro was written to commemorate the Bicentennial of Greensboro 1808–2008. It's a celebration of 200 years of history, tradition, and progress in the piedmont county seat. The images show the evolution of Greensboro and the great strides the town made in becoming a trading center and now the third-largest city in the state. It is a great place to live. Greensboro has it all—beauty, quality of life, and educational and economic opportunity. In the beginning, Greensboro was a hamlet in the wilderness backwoods of North Carolina in an area known as the Pine Barrens. The town grew slowly over the first 60 years. John Motley Morehead, its most prominent citizen and governor of the state, had the vision to construct a railroad across North Carolina from the coast to the mountains. After tracks crossed Greensboro, the town emerged as a trading center.

The Civil War stopped all progress as the area lost its male population to the war efforts. Commerce was replaced by troop trains and women and children working the fields. An uphill battle for economic recovery began during Reconstruction. In the period between 1867 and 1895, great progress was made in reconstructing the railroad, the development of public education, and the establishment of five colleges. In 1895, Greensboro reached city status. With 100 trains a day crisscrossing the city, business people were encouraged to locate in an area where raw materials and finished goods could be easily transported.

The city is the third-largest metropolitan area in North Carolina. Because of its vast transportation arteries serving trucking, railroads, and airplanes, it has held its own in trade and commerce. Credit goes to 200 years of leadership as the town went through a metamorphosis from backwater to successful city. Leadership through the chamber of commerce and Action Greensboro continues to move the area forward to continue its economic growth and livability.

The late 1990s were painful as the textile industry was nearly decimated by mergers, bankruptcies, and offshore manufacturing. However, the transformation from hard goods to technology and service centers has brought great economic vitality. The redevelopment of old businesses and the addition of the giants of industry such as the American Express Service Center and the Federal Express hub keeps Greensboro vital and gives the community a clear way to the future.

History continues to be part of the texture that is shared and interwoven with the new entrepreneurs who bring their special expertise to bear on the next 100 years. It is with pleasure I add storytelling to the facts, figures, and history in my quest to chronicle our common heritage. Greensboro is part of a bond that forever connects all regions of the state.

CHAPTER 1

UPTOWN, DOWNTOWN

EDUCATIONAL DAY, GREENSBORO CENTENNIAL 1808–1908.

By 1908, Greensboro was a booming city. Elm Street—north and south—was lined with retail shops radiating from Courthouse Square, where the old 1873 court building stood. The centennial celebration brought attention to the growth of the area. It ushered in a modern age of textile manufacturing, transportation, and education. (Courtesy North Carolina Office of Archives and History.)

The 1918 courthouse was built of Mount Airy, North Carolina, granite. The county acquired land facing Ashe Street between West Market and Sycamore Streets. Ashe Street was closed to form a city block and to provide space for future expansion. The old site was sold for the Jefferson Standard Building, and the area became known as Jefferson Square. A new, modern courthouse was built in 1974, even though the old courthouse is still in use.

The Jefferson Standard Life Insurance Company paid $171,000 for the courthouse property and erected a 17-story, U-shaped twin tower at 101 North Elm Street in 1923. It was the state's tallest building and the pride of Greensboro. In 1991, the company constructed a new building with a towering peaked roof adjacent to the old one to house the Jefferson Pilot Corporation. In 2005, Lincoln National Corporation acquired Jefferson Pilot, making the company the largest publicly traded life insurance company in the United States.

Sidney Alderman became an important photographer after he opened his studio in 1896 (foreground). That was the time when the best neighborhoods of beautiful, Victorian, single-family homes were within a stroll of the business center of town. Alderman moved to High Point and developed the largest commercial photography operation in the United States. Over the years, the homes that were part of the city center gave way to progress. (Historic photograph courtesy Les Seaver-Davis.)

14

The city hall and opera house opened in 1900 on the northeast corner of Elm Street and Friendly Avenue. The opera house became the site of local programs, public meetings, and national touring shows. The 1888 fire station can be seen behind facing Friendly (West Gaston) Avenue.

When the Greensboro City Hall was built, it became part of the first city complex and was used until 1926. Center City Park opened on the site December 2006. (Historic photograph courtesy Les Seaver-Davis.)

A new fire station with six bays was constructed in 1926 on Greene Street to accommodate fire trucks rather than hand-pulled or horse-drawn vehicles. By 1955, the city had six sub-stations. Today the old 1926 station has kept the same exterior, even though it is a restaurant within the Marriott Hotel. Now there are 21 fire stations that are convenient for all neighborhoods in the city.

Carnegie Library rear of West Market M.E. Church. Showing New Sunday School Annex, Greensboro, N.C.

The first freestanding library was built by funds from philanthropist Andrew Carnegie. The Carnegie Library of 1904 was behind the West Market Street Methodist Church on the corner of Library Place and West Friendly Avenue. In 1939, the library moved to the Richardson Civic Center, which was opened after the First Presbyterian Church built a new sanctuary. After the move, the West Market Street Methodist Church built a modern education building on the old library site.

The Greensboro Public Library moved into a home of its own on the corner of Greene Street and Friendly Avenue in July 1964. The spacious new building included a separate children's room and an auditorium. The building now houses the Elon College Law School, which opened in the fall of 2006. A technologically advanced library opened in September 1998 on Church Street across the street from the Greensboro Children's Museum.

The first federal government–owned post office building was erected on the southeast corner of Elm and Market Streets at Courthouse Square in 1883. It was considered an important modern addition to downtown. The mail was carried in and out of town by the train a few blocks away. The building was enlarged in 1904 to include a third floor but was outgrown by 1933. Today the Law Center and Greensboro Athletic Center occupy the site.

Post Office, Greensboro, N C.

The grand opening of the modern 1933 post office drew a crowd. It is across the street from the 1918 county courthouse. Today the building is used as a federal court building. By 1955, the city was a regional mail hub. Now there are neighborhood post office branches that coordinate mail with the main post office on Morrow Boulevard. (Historic photograph courtesy the Farrell Collection, North Carolina Office of Archives and History.)

In 1900, the activity on Davie Street bustled with warehouses, manufacturing, and stables. By 1910, the street was paved in cobblestones for a few blocks south from Market Street toward the railroad depot. Today it is the location of new condominiums, the cultural arts center, and restaurants. Modernization is taking over the old structures that have survived. They are repurposed for modern living. The cultural arts center incorporated the old Greensboro News Building, a printing company, and a mattress factory.

When demand for entertainment increased, the Central Carolina Fair was organized in 1900 on a 32-acre site on West Lee Street. Meetings and exhibitions were held as well as the annual fair. Citizens wanted to construct an auditorium as a tribute to those who fought in World War II.

The Memorial Auditorium and a coliseum were built side by side on the fairgrounds site in the late 1950s. (Historic photograph courtesy the Farrell Collection, North Carolina Office of Archives and History.)

COMMERCIAL
ENDEAVORS

The delivery truck for F. H. Krahnke Jr. is parked in front of his location on West Market Street. Krahnke was among the small businessmen who opened in the area close to Courthouse Square. In the 1920s and early 1930s, his location was next door to the old post office. Krahnke made "high grade custom made clothes." (Historic photograph courtesy the Farrell Collection, North Carolina Office of Archives and History.)

The first Belk store was built in 1898 on South Elm Street on the south side of the railroad tracks where the Browsery is today. The second store (pictured) was located on the 300 block of South Elm until a modern, three-story department store was opened in 1955 on Courthouse Square, where Caldwell and Son was constructed in early 1800. The modern Belk in Friendly Shopping Center continues to thrive. (Historic photograph courtesy North Carolina Office of Archives and History.)

In 1900, Ellis Stone Department Store was a prestigious locally owned retail shop with James Allen as president. The building was located on the west side of South Elm Street.

When downtown became the place to be in the early 1950s, they built a bigger, modern store across the street. It is now the site of the Elm Street Center.

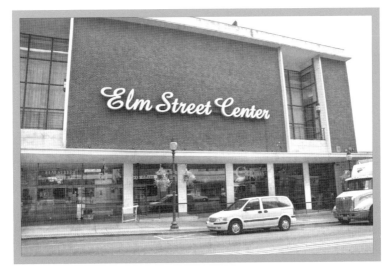

The City National Bank began in 1885 as the Piedmont Bank of Greensboro. It was converted into a national bank in 1899, and a new building was erected on South Elm Street in 1905. Its assets were liquidated in 1908. In the 1970s, two-thirds of the building was razed for widening the street, February One Place. Tons O' Prints is now the sole occupant of the building. (Historic photograph courtesy Les Seaver-Davis.)

McClamroch Mantleworks was opened on the east side of South Elm Street after James McClamroch arrived in 1891 (first building in foreground on left). The family was known for their millwork products as well as fine ceramic tile. In the late 1970s, the property was sold and remodeled as the Mantleworks Restaurant. The restaurant burned and is now a vacant lot waiting for renewal. (Historic photograph courtesy Les Seaver-Davis)

J. Spencer Love of Burlington built Burlington Industries from a single mill to a textile giant. By 1955, the company was the largest weaver of synthetics in the United States and had 90 plants and employed 45,000. The world headquarters moved from the corner of Eugene and Bellemeade Streets to a campus setting on Friendly Avenue. The building was considered the building of tomorrow. It was imploded in 2005. A new shopping center opened on the site in October 2006.

Moses and Caesar Cone purchased vast acreage northeast of Greensboro in the late 1800s. Beginning in 1895, they opened textile mills—Proximity, Revolution, and White Oak. All accessed the proximity of the cotton fields and the railroad to bring cotton in and transport finished fabric out. The White Oak (then image) was the largest producer of denim in the world. It continues production today. The Revolution Mill has been transformed into the Nussbaum Center for Entrepreneurship. (Historic photograph courtesy Les Seaver-Davis.)

Gate City Motors was established in 1914 by C. W. Edwards Sr. on Church Street near the original location of the First Presbyterian Church. When the Lincoln-Mercury dealership moved down the street, the old building stood vacant until it became the site of the Greensboro Children's Museum in 2001. The museum was constructed by repurposing the space within the original structure. Today the museum sponsors hundreds of educational programs for children. (Historic photograph courtesy Gate City Lincoln-Mercury.)

COMMERCIAL ENDEAVORS

The *Patriot* newspaper was published from 1826 until it became a farm publication in 1947. The early office was located at 230 West Market Street. Few newspapers were published during the Civil War. But, despite the war, school textbooks were printed in the old building. Retail shops from the early 1900s now occupy the former site. They are being turned into condominiums. (Historic photograph courtesy Greensboro Historical Museum.)

The *Daily Record* newspaper was established in 1890 in the Benbow Building basement by Harper Elam and Joseph Reece, who owned a printing business. Then it moved to the building on Greene Street shown in the then image. The *Greensboro News* merged with the *Record*. In 1984, the *Record* discontinued publication. Today the newspaper office occupies a modern facility on East Market Street. (Historic photograph courtesy the Farrell Collection, North Carolina Office of Archives and History.)

Southern Loan and Trust Company formed in 1890 as a real estate and rent collection agency. By 1899, their five-story office building at 112 East Market Street was considered the most modern building between Richmond and Atlanta. The insurance division became Pilot Life Insurance Company in 1924. In 1930, Jefferson Standard Life Insurance Company acquired a controlling interest in Pilot Life. This site is now a parking lot. (Historic photograph courtesy Les Seaver-Davis.)

Blue Bell Jean Company started when C. C. Hudson began sewing denim into jeans above a grocery store on South Elm Street. His garments were so popular he built a manufacturing plant down the street and the area became known as Hudson Hill. Blue Bell grew, merged, and became Wrangler. The Wrangler headquarters now occupies a modern building on North Elm Street straight up the street from where it all began.

COMMERCIAL ENDEAVORS

Vicks Chemical Company was founded by Lunsford Richardson, a pharmacist, after he developed a formula for Vicks VapoRub in his drugstore on South Elm Street. He sold his business and began the L. Richardson Drug Company, after which he started Vicks Chemical Remedies. His manufacturing facility was constructed on 21 acres south of Benbow Park on Milton Street in 1924. Proctor and Gamble bought the company and constructed a modern facility on West Market Street that continues to manufacture Vicks products.

Melvin's Sinclair Service Station was one of many gasoline stations dotting the city in the late 1920s. After automobiles became popular, a station was built on nearly every corner within the city limits. Melvin's was located at 1035 West Lee Street. It is now the site of a tattoo parlor. (Historic photograph courtesy the Farrell Collection, North Carolina Office of Archives and History.)

The Army Air Force opened Basic Training Center 10 on March 1, 1943. It was the largest military facility located within a city in the United States. At the end of the war, it became a redistribution center. It was closed in 1946. In the ensuing years, the area included the site of Summit Shopping Center, neighborhoods, and fast food restaurants. Many of the barracks-type structures have been repurposed for a variety of industrial businesses. (Historic photograph courtesy Greensboro Historical Museum.)

Small, rural general store and gas station combinations, like J. T. Bowman's Esso, operated throughout the county from the 1920s into the 1970s. They were convenient one-stop shops for the motoring public before 7/11s. In 2005, Sheetz began constructing gigantic one-stop service stations throughout Greensboro. This one is on the corner of Guilford College Road and Bridford Parkway. (Historic photograph courtesy Farrell Collection, North Carolina Office of Archives and History.)

COMINGS AND GOINGS

Elm Street, north and south, is Greensboro's main street. For nearly 200, years it has been the site of parades and public events, as well as a commercial center. In 1908, the centennial celebration was the largest event the city had ever held. It attracted thousands of people from all over the state to attend church services, musical performances, the march of 10,000 students, and Civil War veterans on horseback. (Courtesy North Carolina of Archives and History.)

On June 9, 1899, the Southern Railroad's three-story depot was constructed on land that was part of the right of way of the North Carolina Railroad. It ran perpendicular to South Elm Street but parallel to the tracks. The structure featured a turret and mansard roof with a covered platform that protected passengers from the elements. A restaurant provided food service for travelers and citizens. Modern condominiums now take the place of the old station.

Southern Depot, Greensboro, N. C.

By 1927, the old station was dilapidated. The opening of a new depot on Washington Street was the biggest event in the city. As the heyday of the railroad faded, so did the depot. Passenger service was moved to a small bleak building off Holden Road. In 2005, the 1927 depot was renovated and restored as a transportation center serving bus and train transportation. (Historic photograph courtesy Farrell Collection, North Carolina Office of Archives and History.)

When steam trains crossed the state, a maze of tracks crossed Greensboro. Over 100 trains a day stopped at the Elm Street depot. Greensboro became known as the Gate City with trains running in six directions. Southern Railway continues to have a large presence with as many as 35 trains a day passing through, including Amtrak passenger trains stopping at the depot. (Historic photograph courtesy Greensboro Historical Museum.)

The first passenger airplane left Lindley Field on November 6, 1930, using a dirt runway, shown in the then photograph. The hangar is behind the plane; the refreshment stand is visible on the far left. The runway was not paved until the Army Air Corp took over the airport during World War II. It is now the Piedmont Triad International Airport. The modern airport terminal was constructed in 1982. (Historic photograph courtesy Farrell Collection, North Carolina Office of Archives and History.)

Walter McAdoo built the McAdoo House at 311 South Elm Street in 1908 as the city's first modern hotel. It was described in advertisements as "a magnificent structure." It had a tall cupola (seen on the right). It had 40 rooms where travelers stayed in luxury. It burned in 1916. Today a parking lot and the outdoor dining facility of Cheesecakes by Alex stand on the site. (Historic photograph courtesy North Carolina Office of Archives and History.)

South Elm Street, Looking North, showing McAdoo Hotel, Greensboro, N. C.

South Elm Street, looking South, Greensboro, N. C.

Dr. D. D. W. Benbow erected the Benbow Hotel at 132 South Elm Street in 1871 at a cost of $40,000. It was one of the first hotels in the prestigious location near the courthouse. It was built of wood and burned in 1899, but was not rebuilt. The Guilford Hotel replaced it, and Dr. Benbow's son built the new Benbow Hotel at another site in 1902. (Historic photograph courtesy Greensboro Historical Museum.)

Guilford Hotel, Greensboro, N. C.

The Guilford Hotel was built in 1900 by B. H. Merrimon to replace the old Benbow Hotel (see page 45). It was considered among the top three accommodations in town after the McAdoo House was built. It was located on the corner of South Elm Street and February One Place. This hotel gave way to the F. W. Woolworth Store, a site of the civil rights sit-in movement. The building is now being renovated as the International Civil Rights Museum.

The O. Henry Hotel was built in 1919 on the southwest corner of North Elm and Bellemeade Streets on the site of Clement G. Wright's home (formerly his grandfather Jesse H. Lindsay's house). Wright led the way in organizing the stock needed to construct the 300-room building. It was razed in 1979. A new O. Henry was opened by Quaintance Weaver on Green Valley Road in 1999. The architect captured elements of the original hotel. (Historic photograph courtesy Les Seaver-Davis.)

The King Cotton Hotel was constructed in 1927 by J. E. Latham, a cotton broker, at the corner of Davie and East Market Streets. This was the site of Christopher Moring's Inn in antebellum days. In its heyday, the 300-room King Cotton hosted meetings, balls, and banquets. When it closed, the property was used as a dormitory for North Carolina A&T University. The building was imploded in 1973. A modern city parking deck now stands on the site.

CHAPTER 4

LIFESTYLE

When C. M. Vanstory Jr. was a teenager, he watched the O. Henry Hotel being built across the street from his home on North Elm Street, as noted in the book *Greensboro 27* by Abe Jones Jr. The rezoning of the property for commercial use was one of the first zoning changes that eventually brought about the demise of the entire neighborhood of magnificent Victorian homes.

Henry Humphreys built a massive, three-story house on the southwest corner of Elm and Market Streets about 1832. He operated a retail shop in the street-level space, and his family occupied the top two floors. Citizens of the town called it "Humphrey's Folly." Over the years, it became the Piedmont House Hotel, the Central Hotel, and business offices. The building was replaced with the First Citizens bank building. (Historic photograph courtesy Greensboro Historical Museum.)

Blandwood Mansion was first constructed as a farmhouse on 12 acres. John Motley Morehead converted it into a Tuscan villa in 1844. After his death in 1866, family members resided in the house for 50 years. In 1897, it housed the Keeley Institute, a clinic for the treatment of alcoholism, pictured in 1899. It was rescued for a historic site in 1973 and remains as the oldest example of Italianate architecture in the United States. (Historic photograph courtesy Les Seaver-Davis.)

John Walker Fry moved into 340 North Elm Street with his wife, Nannie, and three daughters. Elm Street had recently extended to Lindsay's woods to include the new block. In 1917, Fry's daughter, Mary, and her husband, Pierce Rucker, occupied the home. Dr. Wesley Long altered the house next door for a hospital and built an annex. Today the Greensboro Chamber of Commerce occupies a portion of the site of the Fry/Rucker home. (Historic photograph courtesy Les Seaver-Davis.)

J. C. Bishop's beautiful Victorian house was built in 1897 next door to Walker Fry's home at 342 North Elm Street. Among its features were hand-carved trim. The steps and decorative column bases were made from Mount Airy granite. At the time, the block of homes was located within three blocks of Courthouse Square and was a convenient walk to work and shopping. A modern office building now stands in place of these Victorian homes. (Historic photograph courtesy Les Seaver-Davis.)

Lyndon Swaim, the third editor of the *Greensboro Patriot* newspaper, lived in this Gothic-Revival cottage at 113 Church Street. He was one of the few newspaper men spoke against North Carolina's secession from the Union. A modern condominium complex—Governor's Court—is now at the site. It is part of the effort to provide up-scale housing in the downtown area. (Historic photograph courtesy Greensboro Historical Museum.)

In the late 1800s, Lindley Park was considered a wilderness even though it was only a few miles from the city center. That is, until the Greensboro Electric Company built the Lindley Amusement Park and routed a street car to the area. It became a retreat from city life, and weekend cottages were built. After World War II, houses sprang up. The first public swimming pool in Greensboro was built in the park in 1953. (Historic photograph courtesy Les Seaver-Davis.)

A neighborhood sprang up near the Normal and Industrial School (now University of North Carolina at Greensboro) beginning in 1892. Churches and businesses were opened to serve the students and professors. Many houses remain and are undergoing restoration, however much of the area has been incorporated into various college expansions. The Weatherspoon Art Gallery, organized in 1942 as part of the 50th anniversary of the college, was part of the revitalization of Spring Garden Street. (Historic photograph courtesy Les Seaver-Davis.)

The Asheboro Street (now Martin Luther King Boulevard) neighborhoods were a new, upscale area in 1900. Residents were attracted to settle near the businesses on South Elm Street on the south side of the railroad tracks. Asheboro and Gorrell Streets are now undergoing revitalization through efforts of the city and property owners in the development of the South Side neighborhood. Many Victorian homes have been saved. Abandoned houses and vacant lots are the sites of new homes.

Greensboro County Club was founded in 1911 after Alexander W. McAlister introduced the game of golf to Greensboro. McAlister had the idea of building a neighborhood around a golf club and clubhouse. This led to the development of the Irving Park residential area. The clubhouse has undergone many renovations over the years. However, the club and surrounding houses have been preserved.

The Wafco Mill was built in 1891 to produce cornmeal. It was managed by the same family for five generations and was still producing plain and self-rising cornmeal and flour in the 1970s. It was the first company in the state to supply mixed feed for livestock. In the 1980s, the property including the mill building was turned into condominiums. It was one of the first projects involved in repurposing historical buildings.

The original Cone Mills property included hundreds of residences built to house thousands of workers who moved to town to become employees at the Revolution, White Oak, and Proximity Mills. Rent was paid based on the number of rooms in each house. In the 1950s, the houses were sold to mill employees. Today the houses reflect the proud heritage of the mill families. Many owners have modernized the structures by adding porches, room additions, decks, and wrought-iron embellishments.

White Oak Cotton Mills, Greensboro, N. C.

QUALITY OF LIFE

It is thought the first Friends Meeting was established around 1754 in a farming area the Quakers named New Garden. The larger New Garden Friends Meeting was erected in 1791. John Collins of New Jersey sketched a view of this structure showing the schoolhouse on the left where the classes were held for Quaker children and also for slaves and slave children. (From the Quaker Collection, Guilford College Library.)

New Garden Hall, constructed in 1912, replaced the meetinghouse of 1883. The building from 1877 burned. It was used for the New Garden Meeting until the building was made part of the Guilford College campus in the 1970s. The meeting moved across New Garden Road adjacent to the old burying ground that dates back to the years before the Revolutionary War. (Historic photograph courtesy Guilford College Library.)

West Market Street Methodist Church is the oldest Methodist congregation in Greensboro. The third church was built in 1893 (photographed in 1895) on a wide, dirt street lined by Victorian homes and elm trees. In 1918, the county courthouse was built across the street. Although the building looks much the same, the neighborhood has changed dramatically. The modern photograph shows a dynamic city backdrop. (Historic photograph courtesy Les Seaver-Davis.)

First Presbyterian Church began as a church to serve those living within the town limits. The first small, brick building was used as a hospital for Confederate soldiers wounded at the Battle of Bentonville. In the late 1890s, the church was replaced with a large sanctuary and Sunday school wing. This building became the Richardson Civic Center, and a new sanctuary was built on Fisher Park Circle in 1929. (Historic photograph courtesy Greensboro Historical Museum.)

Buffalo Presbyterian Church is the oldest church in Greensboro. David Caldwell, educator and physician, was its minister for 45 years. The congregation used two different sanctuaries between 1756 and 1827. Then the center section was constructed of hand-made brick. In 1919, the David Caldwell building was added to the left, and the Rachel Caldwell building was added on the right in 1952. Services are held every Sunday. (Now photograph by Jim Dollar. Historic photograph courtesy Greensboro Historical Museum.)

At the turn of the century, the first Jewish congregation came together—both orthodox and reform. The cornerstone for Temple Emmanuel was laid in 1923 on the corner of Florence and Greene Streets. In 1949, the Reform congregation retained Temple Emanuel, and the Orthodox members built Beth-David Synagogue. Temple Emanuel was used for 83 years. The congregation moved into the new temple on Jefferson Road in 2006.

QUALITY OF LIFE

Holy Trinity Episcopal Church was formed when St. Barnabas Episcopal Church and St. Andrews Episcopal Church came together. The new sanctuary was constructed on Greene Street in 1910. Later both St. Barnabas and St. Andrews formed new churches in the suburbs. Holy Trinity was renovated in the mid-1990s. The church now retains much of the property on the block. (Historic photograph courtesy of Greensboro Historical Museum.)

ALBERT C. WOODROOF - ARCHITECT -

Walker Street Presbyterian Church was built on the corner of Mendenhall Street and Walker Avenue in 1906 near the campus of the Normal and Industrial School (now University of North Carolina at Greensboro). It became the Presbyterian Church of the Covenant in 1909. The wooden sanctuary was moved to Glenwood. The brick sanctuary constructed in 1916 is still in use as shown in the *c.* 1930 image. (Both photographs courtesy Presbyterian Church of the Covenant.)

West Market Street, looking East, Greensboro, N. C.

The Greensboro Baptist Church became West Washington Street Baptist in 1885 when the members built a sanctuary on the corner of West Washington and Greene Streets. Between 1902 and 1907, they became the First Baptist Church and constructed a new church on the corner of West Market and Eugene Streets near West Market Street Methodist Church (seen in background) and on the omnibus route. It was used until 1952, when a new church was built on West Market Street.

The scene on the 100 block of South Elm was captured by Charles Farrell in 1931. The image focuses north toward Jefferson Square. Liggett's Pharmacy was located on the northwest corner on the first floor of Humphrey's Folly (see page 50) next to the Merit Shoe Company. Beyond, on the southwest corner, is the Jefferson Building. The Now image shows the Jefferson Building is the only building remaining in the scene. (Courtesy North Carolina Office of Archives and History.)

St. Leo's Hospital opened in 1904 on Summit Avenue and was operated by the Sisters of Charity for 49 years. When the hospital closed in 1953, the building became Notre Dame Catholic High School. The last class graduated in 1968. The school was razed in 1970 to make way for urban renewal. Fast food restaurants and an auto store now stand on the site. (Historic photograph courtesy Farrell Collection, North Carolina Office of Archives and History.)

L. Richardson Hospital for Negroes opened in 1927 at Washington Street and Benbow Road as a nonprofit community medical facility. It was a fireproof structure that was well equipped with treatment rooms and an operating room. Dr. C. W. Banner and Mary Lynn Richardson helped raise the funds to build the hospital. It was named to honor Mary Lynn's husband, Lunsford Richardson, the founder of Vicks VapoRub. Today it operates as apartments for senior citizens. (Historic photograph courtesy Greensboro Historical Museum.)

The Sternberger Children's Hospital was donated to the city in 1930 by Blanche Sternberger Benjamin. It opened in the Sternberger family home at 715 Summit Avenue. The facility specialized in orthopedics. In 1936, its services extended to women. When the hospital closed, the building became the location of the Guilford County Department of Public Welfare. Today it is the site of a public park.

Dr. Wesley Long established his first hospital in the Merrimon home (pictured on the left) on the 300 block of North Elm Street, next door to the Fry/Rucker house. Following his death, Long's private hospital was managed by colleagues and became a nonprofit hospital. It moved to its present site on the corner of Elam and Friendly Avenues in the 1960s. It has been enlarged and is now part of the Moses Cone Health Care System. (Historic photograph courtesy Les Seaver-Davis.)

The Green Hill Cemetery land was acquired in 1887 after the city received a $100,000 loan for new streets, a waterworks, schools, and the cemetery. Within 10 years, the hillside was dotted with gravesites. The Eclectic Club purchased lots to rebury the Confederate dead "who still lay in untended trenches," in their words. Today the cemetery stands within the city limits and is crowded with gravesites and monuments. The mature trees cast a pleasant shade. (Historic photograph courtesy Les Seaver-Davis.)

The Moses Cone hospital was planned years before the first brick was laid. Bertha Cone set up a trust when her husband died, with plans for a new community hospital to be built at her death. The hospital was opened in 1953 on Cone land near the Cone Mills plants. The four-story brick structure has expanded many times in the past 57 years. (Historic photograph courtesy the Martin Collection, Greensboro Historical Museum.)

76

CHAPTER 6

EDUCATION

Edgeworth Seminary for young women was founded in 1839 by John Motley Morehead. He was eager for his daughters to have a proper education. He named the school after an Irish author, Maria Edgeworth, who wrote about education for women. It was located near the corner of West Market and Edgeworth Streets. The school closed during the Civil War and was used as a hospital. Classes resumed in 1867, but the school closed for lack of students in 1871.

Immanuel Lutheran College Main Building was constructed on a 13-acre campus on East Market and Luther Streets as a coeducational institution for African American students. It opened in 1905 near the North Carolina A&T University campus. It operated as a four-year theological seminary, high school, and junior college. Today the area is undergoing revitalization with new construction, highway improvements, and beautiful churches. (Historic photograph courtesy North Carolina Office of Archives and History.)

Guilford College was chartered in 1834 and opened by the Quakers in 1837 as New Garden Boarding School. The Yearly Meeting supported the school as a way of filling the educational deficiency in the community. In 1888, it became Guilford College. Founder's Hall, built *c.* 1894, served as the main administration building. Founder's Hall has been rebuilt and is now a student center. (Historic photograph courtesy Les Seaver-Davis.)

Guilford College maintains a beautiful campus in the area once known as the "Village" of Guilford College. The exteriors of the buildings have been well preserved and retain the ambiance of the late 1800s. New dormitories and classroom facilities have been constructed to blend with the older structures. Archdale Hall was built about 1885 and is now used as a faculty office building. (Historic photograph courtesy Les Seaver-Davis.)

Greensboro College was chartered in 1838 as the first school for women in North Carolina. The first section of the Main Building was completed in 1845. It was burned three times but retained its original brick walls. Above is a 1950s view when the building was the centerpiece of the campus with a garden-like appearance. The ivy-covered building has been modernized and is used for offices and receptions. The college is now coeducational.

The University of North Carolina at Greensboro was begun as the Normal and Industrial School for White Girls and opened in 1892. It was renamed the Normal and Industrial College in 1897. The Foust Building was the first structure and was used as offices, classrooms, and dormitories. It became the Woman's College of the University of North Carolina in 1932. Foust is still used. (Historic photograph courtesy Les Seaver-Davis.)

Peabody Park was a barely tamed area of trails and walkways located on the Normal and Industrial School property. When the school was constructed a few miles from town, the wooded area had to be cleared for the first buildings. The image illustrates the natural area that prevailed during the first years. The modern photograph shows that 114 years of constructing roads and buildings has connected the campus to the city of Greensboro. (Current photograph by Jim Dollar.)

North Carolina Agricultural and Technical University began as a college for African American males. The administration building was built with the help of students; some made brick on the property in exchange for tuition. The R. E. McNair Engineering Hall is one of the many modern buildings. It is dedicated to Dr. Ronald E. McNair, astronaut and scientist, who died in the 1986 *Challenger* explosion. The university is now open to males and females and includes international students and faculty.

THE LONG WALK, BENNETT COLLEGE
WITH PFEIFFER HALL IN THE FOREGROUND

Bennett College began as a day school for African American students at St. Matthews Methodist Church in 1873. In 1875, Dr. Edward Thayer became principal and added theology to the curriculum. The Methodist Episcopal church purchased the first 20 acres for the construction of a school with dormitories for high school and college education. Lyman Bennett of New York funded the school, and it became Bennett Seminary in 1881 and then Bennett College for Women. The Pfeiffer Building is the center point of the "long walk." Coeds continue that walk today.

Guilford Technical Community College was established in 1955 on the land where the Central Carolina Tuberculosis Sanitarium once stood. The sanitarium was razed to make way for the community college campus, which was developed to give job training and add skilled workers to the local job force. Now there is a sprawling campus with 4,000 students and many programs, including those for an associate degree. (Both images courtesy Guilford County Technical Community College.)

PRESERVATION

The William Paisley house, built in 1820, stood outside the town limits. Its yard encompassed an entire block. Robert M. Sloan, Paisley's son-in-law and Greensboro's first mayor, lived there. Then it became the home of Dr. John E. Logan. Despite efforts to save it, the house gave way to progress in 1933 when the new post office was built across the street from the county courthouse. (Photograph courtesy North Carolina Collection, University of North Carolina Library at Chapel Hill.)

Rev. David Caldwell performed surgery in the Francis McNairy House on soldiers felled at the Battle of Guilford Courthouse in 1781. Andrew Jackson read law with McNairy's son and lived there prior to receiving his law license on November 20, 1787. The structure was restored and moved to the Mary Lynn Richardson Park adjacent to the Greensboro Historical Society. It is open for tours. (Historic photograph by Mary G. Canfield, North Carolina Collection, University of North Carolina Library at Chapel Hill.)

The third First Presbyterian Church building was built in 1890. When the congregation moved into its present sanctuary in 1931, the old church became the Richardson Civic Center, housing the public library, the museum, and meeting rooms. Greensboro Historical Museum took over the library space when the library moved. The current image shows the outside of the structure, including the J. Henry Smith Memorial Building on the right. The museum added a reception area, a theater, and well-organized exhibits.

The First Presbyterian Church was formed in 1824 by the first group to worship within the city limits when Rev. William D. Paisley preached in the Greensborough Academy Chapel. The church grew from a membership of eight whites and four African Americans. The 1832 building was replaced in 1849. The third church is now the Greensboro Historical Museum. The then image shows the interior of the large sanctuary. Now the same space houses the museum's vast collection. (Historic photograph courtesy Les Seaver-Davis.)

The city limits of Greensboro encompass the Guilford Courthouse National Military Park, the place for Fourth of July celebrations since the beginning of the 20th century. Once located six miles from the city, it was accessible by train. Park headquarters began in a small building and moved into a house before a facility for exhibits was erected. The rangers and interpreters present programs. The battleground trails and bicycle paths are easily accessible. Many commemorative statues are spread throughout the park.

In the late 1800s, trains transported Greensboro citizens from downtown to the Guilford Battleground (now Guilford Courthouse National Military Park) to celebrate the 4th of July. The Then image from 1930 shows such a gathering. The Guilford Battleground Company was established to preserve the battleground and its history. Reenactors now commemorate the battle and present programs on holidays including the anniversary of the battle, 4th of July, and Veterans Day. (Historic photograph courtesy North Carolina Office of Archives and History.)

On February 1, 1960, African American freshmen from A&T University staged a sit-in at the whites-only lunch counter in the Woolworth store. The photograph shows the "Greensboro Four" entering the store. Their protest furthered the progress of the civil rights movement. In 2002, a statue was erected on the A&T campus in front of the Dudley Building as a tribute to the men: David Richmond, Franklin McCain, Ezell Blair Jr., and Joseph McNeil. (Historic photograph by Jack Moebes, courtesy *Greensboro News and Record*.)

In 1931, North Greene Street was a mixture of businesses and homes. The Standard Oil of New Jersey station was a block from the fire station and two blocks from the Fisher Park neighborhood. It was the gathering place for the annual Christmas parade. The float was sponsored by the chamber of commerce and the Merchant's Association and featured Miss Greensboro. Perry's Exxon Service Center is now on the site. (Courtesy Farrell Collection, North Carolina Office of Archives and History.)

PRESERVATION

The World War I Memorial Stadium opened in 1926 on the corner of Lindsay Street and Summit Avenue as a living memorial to citizens who died in the war. By 2004, it was the oldest park in continuous operation used by a minor-league baseball team. The Greensboro Bats finished the 2004 season there before becoming the Grasshoppers and moving into state-of-the-art First Horizon Park on the edge of downtown. (Historic photograph courtesy North Carolina Office of Archives and History.)

Across America, People are Discovering Something Wonderful. *Their Heritage.*

Arcadia Publishing is the leading local history publisher in the United States. With more than 3,000 titles in print and hundreds of new titles released every year, Arcadia has extensive specialized experience chronicling the history of communities and celebrating America's hidden stories, bringing to life the people, places, and events from the past. To discover the history of other communities across the nation, please visit:

www.arcadiapublishing.com

Customized search tools allow you to find regional history books about the town where you grew up, the cities where your friends and family live, the town where your parents met, or even that retirement spot you've been dreaming about.

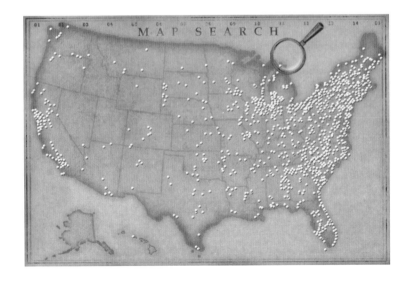